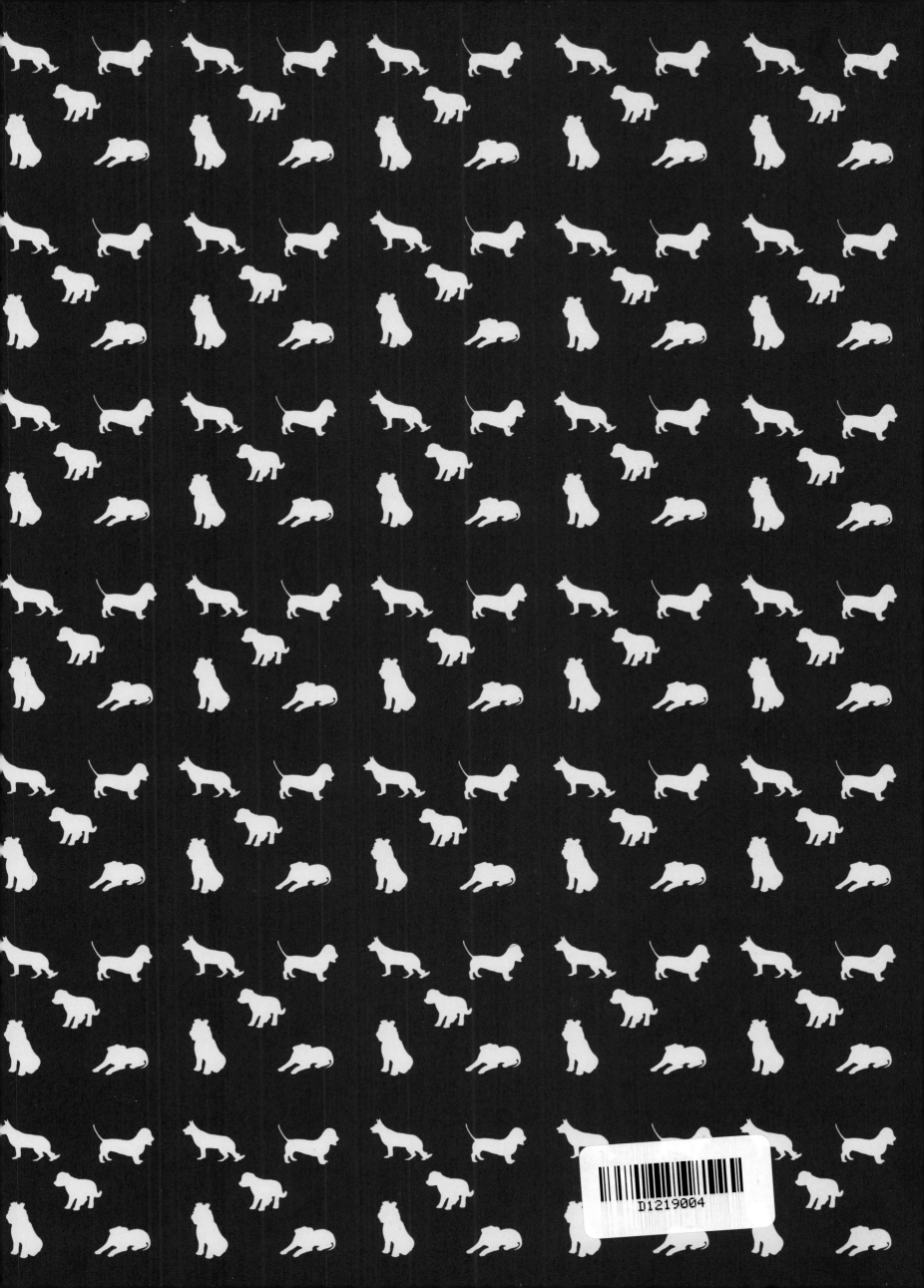

THE WORLD OF
Dogs

THE WORLD OF
Dogs

Angela Rixon

Acropolis
Books

This edition exclusively distributed
in Canada by Book Express
an imprint of
Raincoast Books Distribution Limited
112 East 3rd Avenue, Vancouver
British Colombia V5T 1CB

Distributed in Australia by
Treasure Press

ISBN 1 873762 18 6

Editorial Director: Joanna Lorenz
Project Editor: Clare Nicholson
Assistant Editor: Charles Moxham
Designer: Edward Kinsey

Typeset by MC Typeset Limited
Printed and bound in Italy by
Rotolito Lombarda s.p.a., Milan

The Publishers would like to thank the following photographic libraries for their kind
permission to reproduce their photographs:

(Abbreviations: b = bottom, m = middle, t = top, r = right, l = left, i = inset)
Animal Photography/Sally Anne Thompson 14t, 19, 22, 30, 44t, 44b, 45t, 45b, 47, 50,
62i, 66, 67i, 67, 68, 71, 73b, 78t, 80t, 86b and 90. Animal Photography/R Willbie 1,
13, 26, 43, 51, 69tl and 69b. Barnaby's Picture Library 22i. Bruce Coleman Limited/Jane
Burton 9b, 10t, 33 and 37. Bruce Coleman Limited/Peter Davey 37i. Bruce Coleman
Limited/Nicholas de Vore 83. Bruce Coleman Limited/Bob Glover 18. Bruce Coleman
Limited/Dr Eckart Pott 82. Bruce Coleman Limited/Fritz Prenzel 27, 36 and 62/63. Bruce
Coleman Limited/Hans Reinhard 2, 8b, 14b, 16, 17b, 23, 32, 46, 52, 55, 56b, 57t, 58b,
58t, 59t, 60t, 60b, 61t, 61m, 70, 74t, 75 and 79b. Marc Henrie 34m, 38, 53, 57b, 69tr
and 91. Solitaire Photographic 5, 7, 8t, 10b, 21, 35m, 35b, 39, 41, 49b, 72b, 74b, 80b
and 81. Spectrum Colour Library 11, 12, 34b, 48i, 49t, 49m, 76 and 77. Survival Anglia
88b. Zefa 3, 6, 8tr, 9t, 15t, 17t, 20, 24, 25, 28, 29, 29i, 31, 34t, 35t, 40, 42, 56t, 59b,
60, 64, 72t, 73t, 78b, 79t, 84, 85, 86t, 87, 88t, 89, 92, 94, 95 and 96.

Page one: A Yorkshire Terrier.

Page two: The Dalmatian is a happy, lively and generally
long-lived dog.

Page three: The extrovert and rather mischievous Tibetan
Terrier needs daily grooming to keep its coat in condition.

Page five: Miniature Schnauzers.

CONTENTS

How Dogs Behave

*D*ESPITE THOUSANDS of years of domestication, not all dogs are passive pets. The reasons for aggression and fighting, whether against other dogs or against humans, show a strong link with the behaviour pattern of the wild-dog pack, where fighting is to establish status within the pack rather than to threaten life. Happily, few domesticated dogs fight seriously, their tendency being towards submission. Mock battles occur, just as in the wild, but they rarely lead to serious harm. Such fights customarily end with one dog assuming a dominant posture, the other a submissive pose.

Opposite All dogs enjoy running around off the lead. They should be taught to return to their owner when called.
Below The attitude of this Corgi and the position of his ears shows he is happy at being praised.

In the wild, canine behaviour consists of hunting, eating, sleeping and breeding. The domestic dog's day follows very similar lines, although hunting is replaced by exercise periods and food is provided by the owner. The owner's family becomes the dog's "pack".

Opposite top An English Setter takes a well-earned rest.
Inset Big dogs often need a great deal of exercise.
Opposite bottom An obedient dog is a credit to his or her owner and a pleasure to be with.
Left Most dogs enjoy chewing on a natural bone, and may become aggressive if it is taken away from them.
Below A bitch will often show her natural maternal instincts by mothering the young of another species.

A MEMBER OF THE PACK

*W*ATCHING SOCIAL reactions between dogs can be quite fascinating, and some dogs form very close bonds of friendship. When strange dogs meet they perform a set of ritual behaviours determined by the relative size, seniority and sex of the two dogs. Other factors contributing to the behaviour pattern include the territory on which they meet and whether or not they have met before and managed to establish which is of senior rank.

Above Doggy friends, even if of quite diverse breeds, will happily exercise and play together.
Opposite Two dogs from the same household often indulge in mock superiority battles – just for fun.
Below Two strange dogs meeting on neutral territory approach one another with stiff legs and raised tails.

DOGS AND OTHER ANIMALS

*I*N THE same way that dogs evolved characteristics which allowed domestication, many of them have developed a tolerance and even liking for animals of species which would, in different circumstances, be regarded as enemies or prey. In the earliest days of their alliance with human beings, dogs learned that other domestic animals were an extension of the human family, and accordingly were to be treated with respect.

Once this had been established, over the course of time dogs gradually became humans' allies in hunting and herding, also taking on the function of guard. The human assumed the role of pack leader, and the dog, with its natural wish to please its superiors, was quick to learn which natural behaviours were pleasing and which were not.

Opposite Gundogs make particularly good friends with horses and ponies. Puppies soon learn to keep away from hard hooves and, when they mature, can accompany the riders for exercise. *Above* Puppies and kittens raised together from an early age often become inseparable friends for life.

Opposite above A German Shepherd uses its inborn herding instincts to round up the hens for the night. Many herding breeds naturally round up all manner of creatures – even small children, who may be gently nudged back to the security of a parent by a caring family dog.

Above Dogs can often be extremely inquisitive.

Left Some creatures are not too pleased about being herded. Here a goose shows its displeasure by hissing at a rather unconcerned farm dog.

FETCHING AND CARRYING

*T*HE NEED to carry prey in the wild led to an instinctive ability in the dog to carry objects for its master. This trait was exploited during the early development of the Gundog breeds. In due course dogs emerged that would not only carry game but find it, and then bring it to their master.

Opposite As this German Shepherd shows, aside from the Gundogs many other breeds show an aptitude for retrieving.
Left Spaniels are superb retrievers and also love water.
Below The German Shepherd is an intelligent breed.

YOU, THE PACK LEADER

NO DOG can live a completely carefree existence, of course: it must accept a certain number of simple rules which must be obeyed at all times. It is the dog's innate desire to please you, the "pack leader", that enables it to be trained to follow a wide range of commands.

Each owner has his or her own expectations from a pet dog. One may require just a contented companion, while another may want it to compete in dog shows or tests of training such as obedience or agility contests. Some owners prefer to own a dog of a specific breed that needs specialist grooming, so that they may enjoy all the bathing, brushing and extra care they need to give. Others may require a dog that is an effective guard. There is a type of dog for every purpose.

Opposite The Rough Collie's coat can become quite matted and dirty after a long, muddy walk.
Above The Border Collie is a working dog that needs a considerable amount of exercise and mental stimulation in order to stay fit and happy. It is always eager to please its owner and so makes an ideal pet for training.

Young, active dogs need lots of exercise and enjoy careful training followed by periods of play with their owners. In this way loving bonds are established which remain firm throughout the dog's lifetime.

Teaching your dog to come to call and to obey simple commands can all be made part of the play process. It is usually necessary merely to rebuke a young dog if it is disobedient. Since the only aim of a happy dog is to please its owner, whom it regards as its pack leader, a displeased tone of voice is a perfectly sufficient punishment.

Once the dog is controllable by voice at a distance, it can enjoy free exercise off the lead. You must ensure, however, that your dog will always return to your side on command, in case a potentially hazardous situation suddenly arises.

Above Large active dogs need plenty of exercise, preferably off the lead, and benefit greatly from being allowed periodically to run at speed over suitable open ground.
Opposite The Dalmatian is a breed originally developed to run with and guard horse-drawn carriages. It requires a lot of exercise to keep fit and in good condition.

THE ACUTENESS OF THE SENSES

HE CANINE sense of smell is perhaps a hundred times more sensitive than a human being's, and a dog uses its nose all the time, testing every scent that comes its way. It is this sense that enables dogs to track and to hunt.

Hearing is another canine "super-sense", and a dog's ears are able to pick up very high-frequency sounds. You will often find that your dog becomes excited and gets ready to warn of an intruder long before anyone else has heard the footsteps.

Opposite A dog uses combinations of senses to analyse the elements of its environment and help determine its responses to them. Smell and hearing are acute, and sight is well developed. *Inset* The Corgi is a very game dog considering its small size. *Below* The dog's olfactory acuteness has been put to many uses, such as finding prey, routing out drugs and hunting down criminals.

DIGGING

*W*ILD SPECIES of dog, like the Jackal, often bury parts of their prey to eat later. It is interesting to see how the same behaviour patterns exist in pet dogs, even after many centuries of domestication and even when the dog receives nourishing meals fed to a regular routine.

Opposite Digging in sand is great fun. This dog has probably detected some seaside creature below the surface.
Below Determined to reach a fugitive rabbit, a Spaniel digs under tree roots.

As well as to bury food, a dog will also dig to find it –
for example, to unearth a prey animal that has dived
for safety into its burrow. Some dogs – the members of
the Terrier group – have been bred specifically for
digging out other animals. The name "Terrier" comes
from a French word derived from the Latin *terra*,
meaning "earth".

Most dogs enjoy digging. Search and rescue teams
exploit this trait. When a mountaineer is lost, the dogs
first use their strong sense of smell to locate the person
and can then dig through even quite a heavy covering
of snow and ice to extricate the unlucky climber.

Above This Norfolk Terrier is determined to dig out a wood
mouse hiding under some leaf litter.

TAKING TO WATER

*S*OME DOGS are particularly fond of water; others are miserable even in a light shower of rain, and will do almost anything to avoid stepping in a puddle. Dogs of the Gundog group generally take to water without any problems, and breeds used for police and army work need to accept water as a natural environment.

Below This German Shepherd is thoroughly enjoying its paddle in deep water, and is waiting expectantly for a stick to be thrown for retrieval.

Sporting dogs must obviously be as happy to work in water as on land. Field trials are held for various sporting breeds, and for the retrieving dogs these are run as closely as possible to a normal day's shooting: the dog is required to fetch fallen game, shot by the hunt from both land and water, gaining points for speed and expertise. Dogs chosen to compete in such trials must be not only totally unafraid of water but accomplished swimmers. Most are taught to enjoy such activities from a very early age.

Opposite A Munsterlander is a good all-round gundog which works well in water and is an admirable retriever.
Opposite inset Swimming will give a dog more exercise than an equivalent period of running.
Below Some dogs enjoy sailing and settle down to a life afloat. As well as being good companions, they make effective guards.

Some types of dog have a naturally waterproof coat, the water being kept from saturating the hair by lanolin, an oil secreted by the skin to protect the undercoat. On leaving the water they can shake off most of the water collected in the coat, and soon dry off completely. Other types can become quite waterlogged and must be watched in case they encounter difficulties when swimming.

All dogs should be encouraged to shake themselves when they come out of water, and delicate dogs should be dried thoroughly with a rough towel, paying particular attention to the head, neck, legs and paws.

Opposite A trio of Norfolk Terriers wades right into a flowing stream in order to drink after exercise.
Below Dogs are able to shake their bodies very vigorously after swimming in order to remove excess water from their coat.

Puppyhood

THE TERM "puppy" describes a young dog from the time of its birth until the age of about one year, when it becomes an adult. Newborn puppies are blind and helpless and almost deaf, and are totally dependent upon their mother. Over the next twelve weeks each little dog undergoes a rapid period of growth and development. For the first ten days the puppy only suckles and sleeps, being kept clean by its mother, who licks it regularly to keep it spotless. At this age the puppy makes only quiet noises and is unable to raise itself up on its legs.

Opposite This little Chow Chow puppy is somewhat uncertain about life in the big, wide world outside.
Below Most puppies are still unsure of themselves at six weeks of age, and must be encouraged to venture away from their mother.

Above At eight weeks a puppy is fully weaned and may be ready to go to its new home. This Munsterlander puppy is exploring the sand pit.
Right Young puppies do not venture far from the rest of their litter.
Below A delightful pair of nine-week-old Golden Retriever puppies.

Top The mother is always tolerant of her pup's exuberance.
Above This little Boston Terrier has quickly adapted to playing outside, happily romping with his new owner on the lawn.
Left Summer is the ideal time to acquire a new puppy, because it can spend its exercise periods out of doors.

35

LEARNING TO SOCIALIZE

A PUPPY'S EYES open when it is between ten and sixteen days old, but it will still be unable to focus them properly for a few more days. At this time its body and leg muscles strengthen, so that it is able to raise itself up and move both backwards and forwards. Soon it will start to explore the area away from the whelping box. Between three and ten weeks of age a puppy is weaned and goes through further learning processes: it begins to play with its litter-mates and its mother, and learns to socialize with humans.

Above A gentle Boxer bitch still nurses her puppies although they are old enough to be fully weaned.
Opposite This tiny Schipperke (Belgian Barge Dog) puppy still has baby-blue eyes at three weeks of age. This colour will change as the puppy grows older.
Inset It is unusual to see puppies with both parents. Male dogs do not take any part in the rearing of their offspring.

During the socialization period, when they are between three and ten weeks old, puppies play quite happily together. There is usually a fair degree of mock fighting, with accompanying yapping and growling. Now and again, however, a real fight breaks out following some extra roughness by one of the puppies during play. By this time the teething process is well under way, and the puppies are capable of nipping quite sharply. Those sharp teeth also encourage the mother to cooperate with you in weaning the litter onto solid foods, as suckling is now painful for her.

Opposite Puppies love to test their sharp new teeth on everything. These Border Terriers are chewing on tough plastic flowerpots in the garden . . .
Above . . . but this little Boston Terrier prefers to sniff a pansy.

CHOOSING YOUR PUPPY

C HOOSING THE right puppy needs serious thought and careful consideration. Puppies can be very appealing, and it can be difficult to resist taking on such a delightful little creature, but you should never buy a puppy on impulse alone. You are buying a dog, not just a puppy. Within a year that tiny puppy will be a mature dog, with an average life expectancy of about twelve or thirteen years. During all this time it must be fed, cared for, properly exercised and regularly vaccinated.

Below Selecting a puppy from the litter is just the first step in acquiring a pet which will soon become an adult dog.

Once you have decided you really do want a dog, you must find out about the characteristics of the various breeds and types, so that the dog you choose is the right one for you and your lifestyle. Check out the care and exercise your preferred breed requires, and ensure you will be able to maintain your pet correctly. Ask yourself whether you want a dog as a pampered pet, as a companion for long country walks or as a guard, and make sure the breed will fulfil your expectations.

You must also be certain that you will be able to give the dog all the necessary trimming and clipping that the breed requires to keep up its appearance and ensure its well-being. If you do not have much leisure time, be sure you choose a dog with an easily maintained coat.

Above A Labrador Retriever puppy exploring its new home. This breed is sturdy and generally has a good temperament, and a bonus is that its coat is easy to groom.

It is also important to decide whether you want a dog or a bitch puppy. Especially in the larger breeds, male dogs are generally outgoing and more aware of life in general, while bitches tend to relate rather better to the family and the home. In smaller breeds the differences between the sexes are less marked.

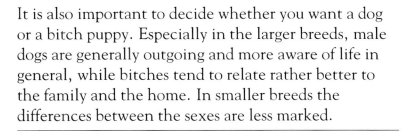
Opposite Picking a pet from a litter of virtually identical puppies may require the breeder's expert assistance.
Above These romping Shar Pei puppies are quite delightful. It can be hard, when confronted by such enchanting creatures, to keep it in mind that this is a very specialized breed, and that these dogs will need expert knowledge and care for the whole of their lives.

Ordinary puppy play can be destructive. Terriers like to dig, Gundogs like to carry things around in their mouths, and all manner of objects can be treated as substitute siblings by dogs of any breed.

Puppies of all types need consistent love, care and understanding, and time must be set aside to teach them right and wrong. A puppy in its new home will quickly learn that praise and petting reward acceptable behaviour, while naughtiness earns a swift rebuke.

Right A Border Collie puppy is unsure about his new toy.
Below This Dalmatian is having a fine time romping in the garden.

Left A true Terrier, this Norfolk puppy is digging up freshly sown seeds.
Below Gundog puppies like this English Setter naturally learn to retrieve.

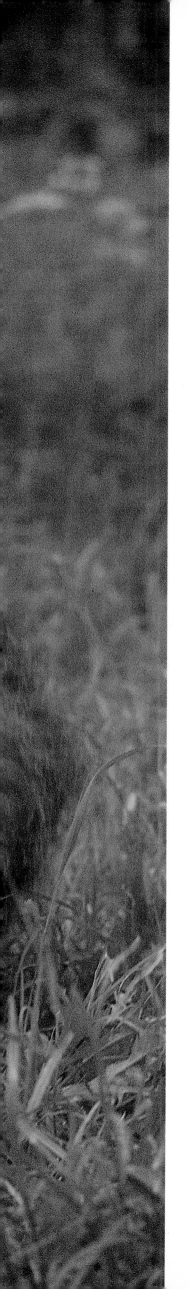

All Sorts of Dogs

*D*OGS COME in an amazing diversity of breeds, ranging from the diminutive Chihuahua to the giant Great Dane. They can also be categorized in terms of their coats, from virtually hairless breeds like the Chinese Crested to Sheepdogs, with their shaggy coats. Also there are specialist coats, like those of the Poodles.

Basically, however, Kennel Clubs around the world organize dog breeds into groups according to both the role they play in human society and their position in the canine kingdom.

Opposite The Old English Sheepdog (or Bobtail), once a weatherproof herding dog, is now a popular pet breed.
Below The loyal and affectionate Bulldog is good with children and needs very little exercise.

Opposite This typically spotted Dalmatian is enjoying his daily exercise.
Inset The Lurcher, a crossbred variety derived from a mixed Hound crossed with a Working Dog, is used for coursing.
Left West Highland Terriers make happy, healthy housedogs, though their coats need considerable care.
Left below The Bull Terrier makes an excellent guard dog. It is easy to groom but requires careful early training.
Bottom The Pointer is a member of the Gundog group. It excels in the field, and makes an affectionate, easily trained housedog, gentle both with children and with other pets.

TERRIERS

*M*OST OF today's Terrier breeds originated in Britain, with some of the basic stock being recorded as early as the fifteenth century. By the year 1677, Terriers had been divided into two types: the first was smooth-coated and had short legs, and was used for hunting underground; the second had a weatherproof, wiry coat and longer legs, enabling it to hunt above ground. Both types were renowned for their digging ability and their tenacity in seeking and holding onto their prey. As time went by, each region of Britain developed its own special breed of Terrier, and some of these exist to the present day.

Opposite The Norfolk Terrier is a happy and adaptable dog which makes a good family pet, likes children and responds very well to training.
Above The Dandie Dinmont Terrier is a one-man dog. Courageous and intelligent, it makes a fairly ferocious watchdog but needs plenty of exercise.

The different Terrier breeds were developed for specific roles. Whatever that role might be, fearlessness was the most highly prized quality, and it is a trait still apparent today. Terriers with strong jaws and short legs, like the Dandie Dinmont and the Sealyham, were used as badger hounds; and, when the vogue for dog-fighting started, the best of the pugilistic dogs were bred by crossing Terriers of various sorts with Bulldogs. Dog-fighting eventually became illegal and various hunted animals were granted legal protection. Many working Terriers became redundant, their offspring destined to become show dogs and pets.

Opposite Three inquisitive Fox Terrier puppies.
Below The Cairn Terrier, originally from Scotland, makes a hardy and affectionate family dog.

WORKING DOGS

THE MOST popular pedigree dog in the world is the German Shepherd, or Alsatian, which was developed from the highly intelligent sheepdogs of Bavaria in the eighteenth century. Dogs of this breed are in great demand throughout the world for security, police and military duties, and they excel in obedience work. The breed is marked for its high intelligence and, when reared and trained correctly, these dogs make peerless pets and outstanding, loyal and fearless guards.

This is a large breed to keep indoors, and the coat needs regular grooming.

Right A family of German Shepherds waits alertly for its owner's next command.

Joining the German Shepherd in the Working group are such favourites as the Boxer, the Collie and the Great Dane, guard dogs like the loyal Doberman and the stocky Rottweiler, and that royal favourite, the Welsh Corgi.

Above A brindle-coloured Boxer enjoys splashing through the water.
Right Although originally bred for herding cattle, Corgi's have become popular pets.

NON-SPORTING DOGS

THE NON-SPORTING group of dogs includes a wide variety of breeds, some of which make perfect pets.

Left Dignified and loyal, the Mastiff is a wonderful guard dog but needs lots of space.
Above Always white in colour, the Samoyed is a loyal – albeit sometimes independent – pet.

The tallest of the breeds in the Non-Sporting group is the massive Great Dane. Other large Mastiffs include the brave Pyrenean Mountain Dog, bred to protect flocks from attack by wolves, and the famous Saint Bernard. Also from Switzerland comes the Bernese Mountain Dog, once used by the cheesemakers of Berne to haul small carts.

Below Sturdy Bernese Mountain Dogs.
Right Miniature and Standard Poodles are grouped with the Non-Sporting breeds.

COMMON ANCESTRY

*M*ANY OF the breeds in the Gundog and Hound groups have common ancestors. The earliest dog breeders selected carefully for prized features such as a keen scenting ability and tirelessness. This selection process was repeated again and again, until the desirable characteristics were fixed and a true breed had been developed.

Left Two Weimaraners. This breed is often called the Grey Ghost because of its colour. *Below* A pack of Beagles about to start a day's hunting.

HOUNDS

THE BREEDS in the Hound group have a wide range of differing characteristics. This is because they were all developed to hunt different species of prey in different habitats. Some Hounds, like the Afghan and the Saluki, had to be very fast over open ground and were selected for hunting by sight, while others were carefully bred to depend more on their acute ability to scent their quarry, and to follow trails that might have been left quite some time before. Among breeds with this ability are the Foxhound, the Beagle and the Bloodhound.

Opposite The Irish Setter is a beautiful loving dog.
Above The tallest of all dogs, the Irish Wolfhound was used by Celtic kings to hunt wolves and elk.
Top The aristocratic Afghan, once used to hunt deer and wolves, has now become a glamorous show dog and model.

GUNDOGS

THE GUNDOG group includes all the Pointers; these dogs work by coming to the point, standing rigidly, often with one foot raised, "pointing" to the game with their nose. Also in the group are the Setters, which "set" when they locate game, sinking to the ground and, again, "pointing" with the nose.

Spaniels move game either by putting birds up into the air for the guns or running them along the ground. Retrievers are very strong dogs and work through all manner of rough ground to retrieve fallen game and return it to the hunter.

Left A fine pair of happy gundogs poised and waiting for the command to start work.

Previous page The Saluki is one of the oldest members of the Greyhound family. The coursing dog of the Bedouin, it was used in conjunction with hawks to hunt game, including gazelles, in the desert.
Inset The first Dachshunds were bred with longer legs as scent-hounds, then with short legs to enable them to dig out badgers, foxes and hares that had gone to ground. Today's Dachshunds may be Standard or Miniature in size, and have smooth, long or wire coats.

TINY DOGS

*M*ANY FACTORS are responsible for certain breeds of dog gaining popularity at different times. Today, the high cost of feeding and the fact that dog-owners often live in restricted accommodation mean that very small dogs are much sought after. Many of the tiny breeds need very little exercise. Moreover, they do not eat very much, are generally healthy, and live several years longer than their giant counterparts.

Below The Papillon (or Butterfly Dog) is named for its huge fringed ears. It can be a rather jealous pet.
Opposite The Pomeranian is a miniature dog of the Spitz type.
Opposite inset The Maltese Terrier is the oldest of the European Toy breeds.

Some tiny dogs have been bred to have specialized coats, and these need appropriate care. Luckily, most people who take on such little dogs are totally committed to their welfare and take a great pride in seeing that their pets are always groomed to perfection.

Tiny dogs should never be underestimated. Some have the heart of a Rottweiler lurking inside their miniature frames, and make good watchdogs, letting their owners know in no uncertain terms when strangers are around.

Opposite top left A tiny Yorkshire Terrier relaxes in the summer sun.
Opposite top right An apricot-coloured Toy Poodle shows off its fashionable trim.
Opposite, main picture The Pekinese was retained as the Royal Dog of China for several centuries before being first shown in England in 1893.
Right Once used as a circus dog, the Bichon Frise is intelligent and lively with an even temperament.

Dogs at Work

*E*VER SINCE the early days of domestication, the dog has proved a loyal companion and willing servant of mankind. The working dogs of today play an integral role in many human activities, both at work and at play. They provide valuable assistance in police, security and military work, and offer an excellent deterrent to intruders in the home – in every country of the world, dogs are seen as protectors of property and the family. Large or small, of aristocratic lineage or a crossbreed, dogs have proved themselves to be our best friend.

Opposite The Pyrenean Mountain Dog has long guarded flocks in the high borders of France and Spain.
Below The Heeler is a dog bred to work cattle, and is capable of driving them safely and efficiently over long distances.

Right Originally a mountain rescue dog in the Alps in the eighteenth and nineteenth centuries, today's Saint Bernard is a majestic show dog.

Below A semi-wild desert dog stretches itself as it prepares for self-imposed guard duties at the Temple of Karnak, Egypt.

Left Bred to hunt hares, the Beagle, the smallest of the pack hounds, now makes an energetic and lively pet.
Below The Border Collie is an intelligent and tireless worker.

ON THE FARM

ONE OF the oldest functions of the dog is to herd flocks. Herding is a controlled form of one of the dog's own natural instincts: wild dogs likewise herd as part of the predatory process. In human employ the final part of the process must of course be left out: dogs are trained to suppress their desire to attack and kill.

Above The Komondor has been bred in Hungary for hundreds of years to guard large sheep flocks. It is a big, fierce dog with a heavy sheep-like coat of corded hair.
Opposite Many regions develop their own type of herding dog.
Below A Blue Merle Collie shows how sheep should be gathered.

FOLLOWING THE GUN

*G*UNDOGS AT work are a delight to study and observe. Their history in fact predates the invention of guns, for dogs with the special abilities to find, flush out and retrieve game have been in use for centuries. The first "fowling piece", invented in the seventeenth century, gave hunters the benefit of greater range, but this in itself brought problems. Hunters had to breed and train their dogs to work over longer distances, and had to select them for their ability to retrieve game safely.

Opposite The Labrador Retriever is descended from dogs which came from Newfoundland and were renowned for their retrieving ability. This yellow dog is fetching a grouse shot on the moors.
Below A black Labrador shows its field skills in finding and bringing in a pheasant from far across the river.

As well as excelling in the field, most of the Gundog breeds make very good housedogs, as long as they are given enough exercise to keep fit. The majority have good temperaments and are very easy to train – although few of them make good guard dogs, precisely because they tend to make friends with everyone!

Right A beautiful English Setter out for exercise, and obviously enjoying the fresh air.
Below A Pointer showing the classic pose, with its nose directed at the game ("pointing") and one leg lifted and poised.

ON GUARD

*D*OGS HAVE been used as guardians of the home for many centuries, and special crosses between early breeds were made to produce exceptionally fierce and dangerous dogs for guarding large estates. From those breeds have come some of today's famous working guard dogs, such as the Bull Mastiff, which is easily trained and quite fearless.

Many breeds make good family guards although, generally speaking, breeds which bark at strange noises but which are too small to deter determined intruders are better termed "watchdogs". Most family dogs will try to give protection if danger threatens.

Left A dog will often run forward barking fiercely but not carry out the threat if seriously challenged. If forced into a corner, it may bite out of nervousness.
Below This Terrier clearly shows how even a small dog can stand its ground and act as a strong deterrent to intruders.

FIGHTING CRIME

DOGS ARE used by the police forces of many countries in the fight against crime; they are particularly useful in crowd control and in capturing and detaining criminals. Specialist dogs are used to detect drugs and other substances, such as explosives. These dogs are carefully selected for their potential before being expertly trained to carry out their duties. Like other dogs used in law enforcement, these are fastidiously cared for and kept at the peak of fitness at all times.

Police dogs – at least in civilized countries – are trained to attack only on command, and then specifically to bite and hold the malefactor's forearm. Some dogs are taught to attack under gunfire, and how to avoid being clubbed with a weapon. Despite their efficiency at such tasks, police dogs are essentially gentle by nature, and of course they must be totally reliable at all times.

Opposite During intensive training, police dogs learn to clear high fences, walls and gates . . . but like humans they need time to relax.
Below left A police dog soaring over the long jump as part of its regular exercise routine.
Below Jumping is a good test of fitness and ability. It builds muscle and sharpens the reflexes.

PULLING THEIR WEIGHT

THE TWO main sorts of dogs used for draught work are, first, those of the Spitz group, which developed in cold climates and, second, the heavier Mastiff types found in warmer regions. The Spitzes, the better known of the two groups, include such famous breeds as the Husky (or Eskimo Dog) and the Alaskan Malamute. These dogs have been renowned for generations for their ability to pull heavy sleds and thus help make it possible to live in some remote regions. Even today, with the advent of sophisticated motorized sleds, draught dogs are invaluable in some areas. The Eskimos and some North American Indian peoples depend a great deal on their sled dogs, and teams are also used by the police in the frozen Northwest Territories. Each year a great contest, the Iditarod Trail Race, is run in hazardous conditions between teams of sled dogs over more than a thousand miles, ending at Nome in Alaska.

Opposite This sled dog in Greenland shows the typical Spitz characteristics: rounded skull, sharp ears and muzzle, an exceptionally dense coat and a tail which curls over the back when the dog stands up.
Above A dog team sets off with its driver to check the traplines in the inhospitable Northwest Territories.

Dogs as Pets

*M*OST PEOPLE in Western communities who keep dogs want them purely as pets, rather than for any practical purpose. Why are we as a species so keen on keeping pet dogs? The reasons are not immediately clear; several factors are involved. Certainly our feelings towards dogs may be strongly conditioned during our upbringing. Children are exposed to the attitudes of their family and friends; they are bombarded by a multitude of dogs and other animals romanticized and sometimes humanized in films, on television and in books and comics. Whatever its origins, the man–pet relationship is a strong one, and the dog is by far the most popular pet.

Opposite A cheeky Irish Terrier asks to come in after romping in the snow-covered garden.
Below A particularly appealing gaze from a French Bulldog.

Above All dogs enjoy a good walk in the countryside and, assuming they have been taught to come back on command, should be allowed periods off the lead so that they can run around freely.
Below A Basset Hound yawns preparatory to settling down to sleep after a long walk.

Below Some breeds are very agile and enjoy quite strenuous games. This Whippet has been taught to catch the frisbee thrown by its owner, and does not seem to mind wearing team colours!

During the early days of puppyhood pet dogs learn to socialize, to accept humans and other animals as friends. Lessons learned at this critical time in a young dog's life will last for ever, so now is also the best time to forge the permanent dog-and-owner bond of friendship.

Above This little Dachshund can hardly wait to answer its owner's command of "come".
Right This puppy looks full of good intentions.
Opposite Though tiny, the Yorkshire terrier is a hardy, brave little dog which is also easy to train.

SMALL PAWS, BIG HEART

BECAUSE OF their small size, dogs of the Terrier group are often picked as pets, and most of them admirably fulfil that role. It is important, though, to remember the history of the Terrier: several of the characteristics firmly ingrained in these charming little dogs can be extremely antisocial, and must be specifically trained against. They love to hunt and chase, so you must take care when introducing them to other family pets.

Opposite Originally from Scotland, the West Highland White Terrier is full of self-esteem and makes an active pet.
Below One of the few Terrier breeds to originate outside Britain is the Australian Terrier.

AND WHAT OF THE FUTURE?

*W*HAT FUTURE has the dog in our overcrowded world? The answer must be entwined with the answer to another basic question: what lies in humanity's own future? For it seems that the two species are inextricably bound together, each having a need for the comfort of the other's company. Since the earliest days of the dog's domestication, while people have manipulated its physiological structure by selective breeding, individual animals have taken matters into their own paws with results we can see in every park, supplementing all the recognized breeds with a multitude of mongrel types. However, in every single member of the canine race there is one characteristic that cannot be changed – the unique ingredient that says: I AM DOG.

Above What is he thinking about? Wild ducks? A missing master? All his senses are keenly tuned.
Opposite Perhaps the most glamorous of all dogs is the Afghan Hound, once used for coursing in Afghanistan and now a popular show dog which thoroughly enjoys being given all the care and attention it needs.
Previous page As the largest of the group, the Airedale is often referred to as "King of the Terriers". Bred to combine the best qualities of both Terrier and Hound, the Airedale excels as a guard, and has won fame as a police dog and in times of war.
Following page A Collie is at home in the mountains looking over a Scottish loch.